Health Matters
Hygiene and Your Health

by Jillian Powell

RSVP
RAINTREE
STECK-VAUGHN
PUBLISHERS
The Steck-Vaughn Company

Austin, Texas

Titles in the series

Drugs and Your Health
Exercise and Your Health
Food and Your Health
Hygiene and Your Health

© Copyright 1998, text, Steck-Vaughn Company

Published by Raintree Steck-Vaughn Publishers,
an imprint of Steck-Vaughn Company

Library of Congress Cataloging-in-Publication Data
Powell, Jillian.
Hygiene and your health / Jillian Powell.
    p.   cm.—(Health Matters)
    Includes bibliographical references and index.
    Summary: An introduction to basic hygiene, discussing such aspects as skin, teeth, hair, clothes, and food.
    ISBN 0-8172-4926-5
    1. Hygiene—Juvenile literature.
    2. Health—Juvenile literature.
    [1. Hygiene. 2. Health.]
    I. Title. II. Series: Health matters.
    RA777.P68   1998
    613—dc21   97-3260

Printed in Italy. Bound in the United States.
1 2 3 4 5 6 7 8 9 0 02 01 00 99 98

Picture acknowledgments
Chris Fairclough Color Library 7, 25 top; Northern Picture Library 13; Reflections 15 top; Science Photo Library 5, 15 bottom, 23 bottom, 27, 28 (S. Nagendra); Tony Stone Worldwide 17 bottom (Lori Adamski Peek), 19 (Andrew Syned), 23 top (David Oliver), 25 (MacNeal Hospital), 26 (John Fortunato), 29 bottom (David Austen); Wayland Picture Library 4, 6 (both), 8, 10, 11, 12, 14, 16, 17 top, 18, 19 bottom, 20, 22 middle; Zefa 9, 21 both, 24, 29 top (H. Sochurek).

Contents

What Is Hygiene?

Hygiene is about keeping yourself and everything around you clean. If things get dirty, bacteria can grow and multiply. Bacteria are tiny living things that can be seen only under a microscope. They live in the air and earth, on plants and animals, and on and inside our bodies. Most are harmless but others can cause illness and disease.

Personal hygiene is about keeping your body clean. This includes your teeth, skin, and hair.

Your body helps keep you safe from harmful bacteria. Your eyebrows and lashes keep dirt and dust from getting in your eyes. Your skin helps keep germs out of your body. Little hairs help keep germs from getting into your nose. Your tears and stomach juices contain chemicals that can kill bacteria. You can help your body fight off germs by keeping yourself clean.

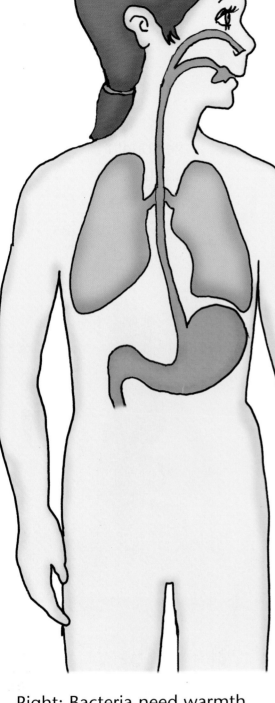

These are some of the ways your body fights germs and disease.

RESPIRATORY SYSTEM

Mucus in nose and windpipe traps dirt and germs. They are carried by hairs to the back of the mouth where they are swallowed.

SKIN

Skin is waterproof and germproof. It repairs itself when you are cut or hurt.

DIGESTIVE SYSTEM

Stomach acid and enzymes destroy germs and bacteria.

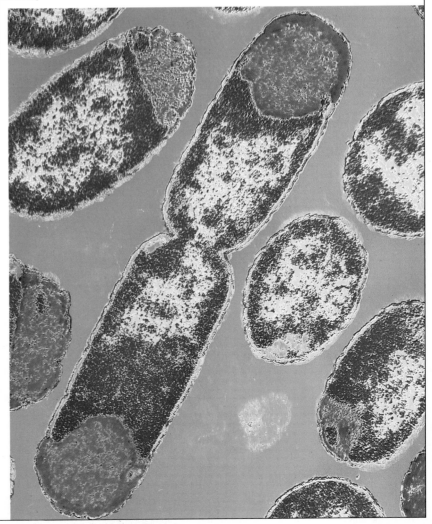

Right: Bacteria need warmth and moisture to grow and multiply. One bacterium can multiply to a million in under seven hours.

Hands Up for Hygiene

It is especially important to keep your hands clean. Dirty hands can spread germs and infections.

During a day, you touch lots of different things with your hands. Dirt and bacteria can get onto your hands and under your fingernails. If these bacteria get onto your food and into your mouth, they can make you sick. You need to wash your hands in warm, soapy water after going to the toilet or touching pets, trash, or dirty items. It is very important to wash hands before touching or eating food. It also helps to keep fingernails short and clean so no germs can hide underneath them.

Use a nailbrush to make sure that your fingernails are clean.

Right: Wash your hands so that germs cannot spread.

Handy rules

Wash your hands
- before touching food
- after going to the toilet
- after doing messy or dirty work
- before touching cuts and grazes
- after touching pets

Right: You should remember to wash your hands after doing messy work like planting seeds in soil.

Washing hands is important for people who work with food in stores, restaurants, and cafés. Design a poster to remind people to wash their hands. You could outline your own hand or make handprints to illustrate it.

Clean Skin

Your skin is very important. It helps keep germs from getting inside your body and keeps it at the right temperature. When you get too hot, skin makes sweat to help cool you down. You can take care of your skin by eating a healthy diet, drinking lots of water, and keeping clean.

Your skin is alive and growing. It is covered with a thin coat of oil that helps it stay flexible and waterproof. Your body makes new skin cells all the time, and dead skin cells flake off. Washing your skin helps get rid of dead skin cells, dirt, and bacteria on your skin. To keep your body fresh and clean you should wash all over every day.

Sponges help you get every part of your body clean.

Try to take a bath or shower every day.

Left: Water and washing are an important part of many religions. In this picture Muslims are washing before they pray. Hindus bathe in temple pools and rivers to make themselves clean. Christians are baptized in water to wash away their sins and to show that they are making a new start.

Keep clean

- clean away the dirt by regular washing
- use a sponge or washcloth to get rid of dead skin
- bathe or shower after using a swimming pool
- keep hands clean so you do not pass on germs

Feeling Fresh

Some parts of your body need special care. You sweat most on your hands and feet, under your arms, and between your legs. Sweat is made by glands in the skin and comes out of tiny holes called pores.

As you get older, your sweat glands start to work harder. If you don't get rid of sweat, your skin can start to smell. This is because bacteria multiply in warm, moist places. The bacteria feed on sweat, dead skin cells, and oils. Then you may start to smell. It helps to wash these parts of your body twice a day and always when you are hot and sweaty after playing sports.

As girls grow up, they need to take special care to stay fresh when they are having their periods each month.

You need to keep your feet clean and dry. Your feet can pick up skin infections like athlete's foot in warm, damp places like swimming pools and showers. You can take care of your feet by making sure you wash and dry them well, especially between the toes, and by wearing flip-flops.

Sweat comes from sweat glands in the skin. As sweat evaporates from the skin, it has a cooling effect because the evaporating liquid carries away body heat

Layers of skin

Sweat duct

Sweat gland

Capillaries to sweat gland

Fat

Sweat contains
water
salt
chemicals

Left: A kind of wart, usually found on the bottom of the foot

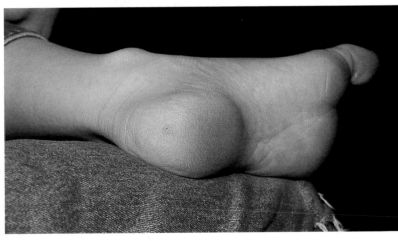

Make a list in words or pictures of all the things we use to keep us clean and fresh. Which do you use every day? Which do you use most days?

Teeth and Hygiene

It is important to keep your teeth and mouth clean and fresh. The adult teeth you grow when you are about six years old have to last you the rest of your life.

When you eat, scraps of food stick to your teeth. Sugar in the food and bacteria in your mouth cover your teeth with a sticky coat called plaque. Plaque contains acids that can eat into the enamel on your teeth. If the acids make a hole, bacteria can get inside and the tooth will decay and need a filling.

Crunchy foods like apples and carrots help keep your teeth and gums clean and healthy.

You can help keep your teeth strong by brushing them after meals and trying not to eat too many sugary foods.

Try to brush your teeth at least twice a day. If you can't brush after every meal, rinse your mouth out with water to help get rid of scraps of food. Some toothpastes contain fluoride, which can help keep your teeth strong.

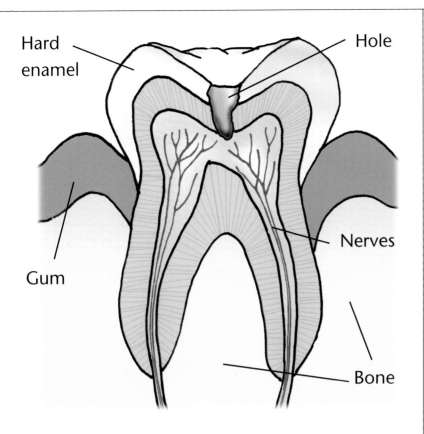

Hard enamel

Hole

Gum

Nerves

Bone

If you eat too many sweet things, germs in your mouth will eat up the sugar, making acid. This destroys the enamel coating on your teeth and makes a hole.

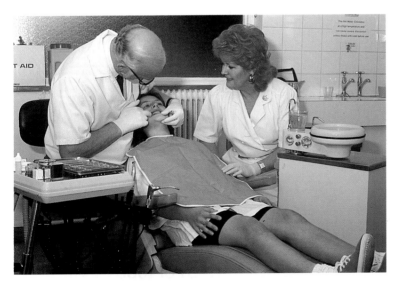

A dentist can help you look after your teeth and show you how to brush them properly. You should visit your dentist twice a year.

Brushing teeth

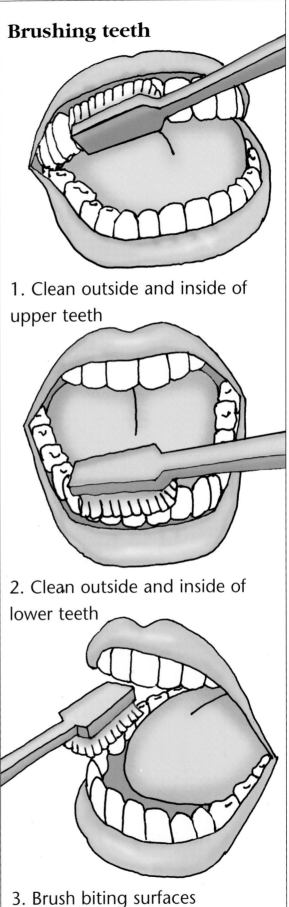

1. Clean outside and inside of upper teeth

2. Clean outside and inside of lower teeth

3. Brush biting surfaces

Squeaky Clean Hair

Hair can pick up dirt in the air. You need to wash it every few days to keep it healthy and clean.

Hair grows out of hair follicles in your skin. Glands around each follicle make oil, which helps your hair look shiny and keeps it from getting too dry.

As you grow up, your hair and skin start to make more oil and can look greasy. Washing your hair gets rid of dirt, oil, and dead skin cells. Choose a gentle shampoo and rub it into your hair well, then rinse in clean water.

Wash your hair regularly using a mild shampoo to keep it clean.

Each hair on your body comes from a hair follicle under the skin.

Hair

Hair follicle

Hair erector muscle

Sebaceous gland

Capillary to hair root

Keep your combs and brushes clean by washing them regularly in warm, soapy water. Don't borrow or lend combs or brushes.

Right: There are tiny insects called head lice that can live in hair. The females lay eggs (nits) that stick to the hair then hatch out into young. Head lice can make your skin itchy and spread easily from one person to another. If you spot lice, brushing and combing may help, or you may need a special shampoo.

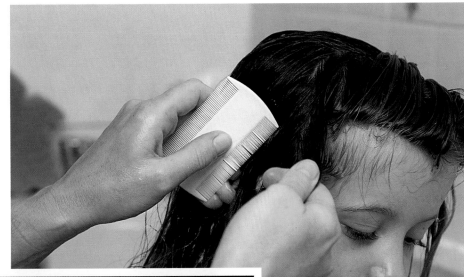

Clothes and Hygiene

You need to change your clothes regularly to stay clean. Some clothes need to be washed more often than others.

As you grow up, you need to change your underwear every day to stay fresh. This is because dead skin cells, oil, sweat, and bacteria can build up and start to make clothes smell. Socks and sneakers can get smelly but some shoes can be cleaned in the washing machine.

In hot weather, it is best to wear clothes in natural fabrics like cotton, because they are woven with tiny holes that let the air through. Cotton underwear helps you stay fresh.

Regular washing keeps clothes fresh.

Left: Cotton is a material that is good to wear in warm weather because it has tiny holes that let the air circulate.

Right: Washing powders and liquids contain detergents that help loosen dirt from fabrics. Stains like grass and oil may need to be cleaned with special stain removers before washing.

Sports clothes need to be washed every time they are used because being active makes you hot and you sweat more.

Hygiene in the Home

Hygiene means keeping the places where you live and work and the things you use clean. Germs and tiny insects can live in dirty homes and make you sick.

Detergents clean dishes by loosening bits of food so they can be washed away.

It is important to keep kitchens and bathrooms clean because bacteria multiply in warm, damp places. Germs live in sinks, toilets, and garbage cans, but they can be killed by disinfectants and other household cleaners. Tiny insects called dust mites live in carpets and bedclothes, feeding on flakes of your dead skin. Dusting, vacuuming, and washing bedclothes regularly help keep the home clean.

Some people have allergies to dust or dust mites, smoke, pollen, animal fur, or feathers.

They can cause
sneezing
runny nose
itchy skin

Left: A dust mite may look alarming but it is tiny. Dust mites like damp conditions in homes and feed on skin.

Right: Regular vacuuming helps keep your home free of dust.

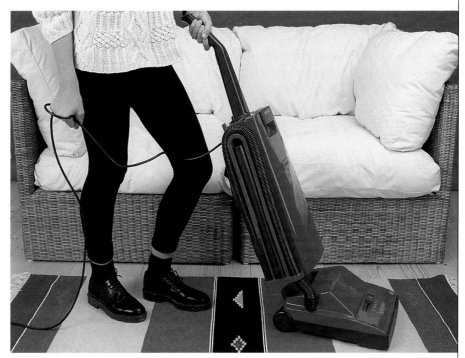

Cut out pictures from magazines showing different cleaning materials and machines. Make a collage called "Clean Homes," that shows how and where the different cleaners can be used.

Food Hygiene

If germs get on your food, they can give you food poisoning. Food poisoning can make you sick for a few days and can be dangerous for old people and babies. Dirty hands and flies can spread germs to food. You should wash raw foods like fruit and salads before you eat them, to get rid of any germs and chemical sprays.

Food may be canned, frozen, dried, or bottled to keep bacteria from growing on it. Food may also contain preservatives to help it last longer.

Bacteria need warmth and moisture to grow, so keeping food in a refrigerator or freezer helps keep it fresh. Raw foods like meat carry germs, so they should be kept apart from cooked foods.

Some foods, including chicken, pork, and eggs, must be cooked thoroughly to kill harmful bacteria. If foods have been frozen, they usually must be defrosted before cooking, or they may not cook through.

Right: Keeping food in a refrigerator or freezer slows the growth of bacteria and keeps it fresh longer.

Prepare food carefully. Some of the most deadly bacteria, such as salmonella, can live in these foods:

Eggs

Dairy products

Above: Remember that sharing food may also mean sharing germs as well.

Poultry

Food Safety rules
● Always wash your hands before touching food
● Keep flies and pets away from your food
● Keep everything in the kitchen clean
● Eat food within "Use by" dates shown on the packages

Find out what happens to samples of bread and milk when they are left out in a warm room. Cover one piece of bread and half a cup of milk and leave them in a warm place for a few days. Check each day and record any changes. What do you think has happened and why?

Pets and Hygiene

If you share your home with pets, you need to think about animal hygiene, too. Some animals, like cats, lick themselves clean but dogs need you to bathe them. Both dogs and cats need to have their coats combed or brushed regularly to get rid of old fur. Sometimes they may need to wear flea collars or have flea powder brushed into their coats to kill fleas living in their fur.

Use flea powder on your dog's fur to get rid of fleas.

Pet rules
- don't let your pet lick your face
- clean your hands after touching or cleaning out your pet's bedding
- keep food for your pet away from the food you eat
- keep your pet clean and free from disease
- give your pet its own toys to play with
- don't let a dog foul grass or sidewalks

You should also try to keep the places where they sleep clean. Animals in cages and birds need to have the straw or paper in their

cages changed regularly. All pets need fresh food and water every day. They should have their own food and water bowls, and these should be washed every day.

Above: Always wash your hands after touching or playing with your pet.

Left: Clean your pet's cage regularly. It will be happier if its living conditions are completely clean.

Right: Animals can carry a skin infection called ringworm. If you catch it, you may have a rash of red, itchy rings on your skin. You will need to use a special cream to get rid of it.

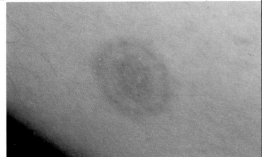

Accidents and Hygiene

If you cut, scratch, or burn yourself, or if an insect bites you, it is important to keep the broken skin really clean, or germs may get into your body and cause an infection.

When you cut your skin, blood comes out. You need to wash the cut under running water, then put on an antiseptic that kills germs. If it is a big cut or graze, you may need a bandage to keep it clean. Deep cuts may need stitches put in by a doctor or nurse.

Below: Your white blood cells help you fight infections by destroying germs. These cells are very, very tiny.

If you cut yourself, the cut must be kept clean. It should be washed and then covered with antiseptic cream and a bandage.

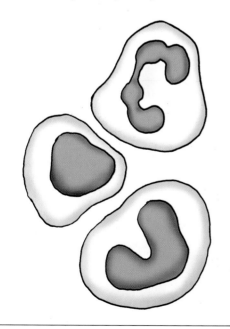

If you burn yourself, hold the skin under cold water for a few minutes, then cover the burn to keep out germs. Bad burns may need to be cared for in a hospital.

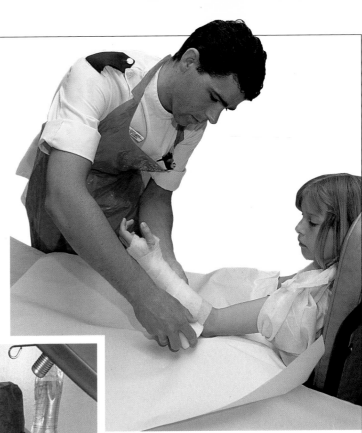

Above: Bandages are carefully wrapped around the body to keep germs out.

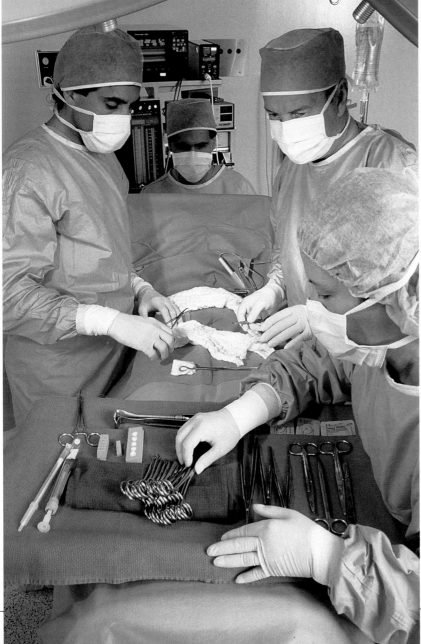

Left: In a hospital, everything must be kept clean and germ-free. During an operation, doctors and nurses wear masks, gloves, and overalls so they don't spread germs.

Bugs and infections

If germs get into your body and multiply, they can make you sick. Cold viruses in the air can get into your body through your nose and mouth. You get a runny nose and eyes as your body tries to wash out the germs with sticky mucus and tears.

Coughing and sneezing are your body's way of helping you clear your nose and throat for breathing when you have a cold. But they can spread germs to others, so you should always use a handkerchief.

When you sneeze, air blows out of your lungs at over 100 mph (150 km/h)—faster than a hurricane!

Left: When you catch a cold, you should stay in and keep warm and drink lots of fluids.

When you are sick, you feel tired because your body needs energy to fight the germs. You need to rest, keep warm, and drink plenty of liquids. Babies and old people need special care when they catch viruses.

The tiniest germs are called viruses. It would take billions of viruses to cover a pinhead. Viruses cause colds and flu as well as illnesses like measles and chickenpox.

These are some of the ways that germs and diseases may be carried

Droplets of moisture

Direct contact or by touching objects

Insects such as houseflies or mosquitoes

Contaminated water and food

Fighting Disease

We need hygiene to keep diseases from spreading. Dangerous diseases spread in countries that do not have clean drinking water and ways of getting rid of toilet waste.

Some diseases can be prevented by immunization. A doctor or nurse injects a vaccine that contains a weak form of the disease. The body makes special germ killers, called antibodies, to fight and kill the disease.

If it comes into contact with the disease later, the body remembers it and can fight it. Babies and children can be immunized against diseases, including polio, tetanus, diphtheria, and whooping cough.

All over the world children are immunized against many dangerous diseases.

Right: A magnified picture of HIV. AIDS is a disease caused by HIV. The virus enters the body in blood or other body fluids. It can be passed on by people sharing dirty needles used to inject drugs or by having sex without using condoms. The virus attacks some types of white blood cells and destroys them so the body cannot fight infections and the person becomes sick.

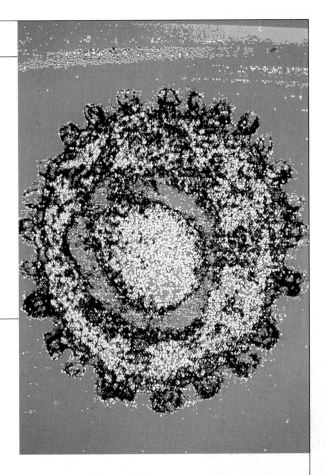

Below: Children in Thailand collecting clean water from a well to load onto carts. A supply of clean water helps prevent disease.

Glossary

Allergy A sensitivity of the body to something from outside, like certain foods, dust, or pollen.

Antibodies Special germ killers made by the body to fight infections.

Bacteria Tiny living things. Some are harmless but others can cause illnesses.

Condoms Protection used to stop pregnancy and AIDS being passed on by an infected person during sex.

Defrosted Thawed so no ice is left.

Fluids Liquids.

Fluoride A substance that helps keep teeth enamel strong.

Glands Cells in the body that form oil, sweat, and other substances.

Immunization Giving a vaccine to prevent disease.

Infections Disease or illness caused by germs entering the body.

Microscope A device scientists use to look at objects that are too tiny to see with the naked eye.

Mucus A sticky substance made inside the body.

Parasite A living thing that lives on something else.

Period The monthly shedding of blood from the bodies of older girls and women if they are not pregnant.

Pollen The fine powder made by flowers.

Preservatives Substances added to food to help it last longer.

Vaccine A weak form of a disease used for immunization.

Books to Read

Bennett, Paul. *Keeping Clean.* (Nature's Secrets.) New York: Thomson Learning, 1995.

Catherall, Ed. *Exploring the Human Body.* (Exploring Science.) Austin, TX: Raintree Steck-Vaughn, 1992.

Cobb, Vicki. *Brush, Comb, Scrub: Inventions to Keep You Clean.* New York: HarperCollins Children's Books, 1993.

Gay, Kathlyn. *They Don't Wash Their Socks!* New York: Walker and Company, 1990.

Nottridge, Rhoda. *Care For Your Body.* (Staying Healthy.) Parsippany, NJ: Silver Burdett Press, 1993.

Index

AUG   1998